Gra the Doll, the Carp, and Me

by Catherine Murphy

✍

illustrated by Rebecca Bond

Scott Foresman

Editorial Offices: Glenview, Illinois • New York, New York
Sales Offices: Reading, Massachusetts • Duluth, Georgia
Glenview, Illinois • Carrollton, Texas • Menlo Park, California

"Take the pass, Yuji!" yelled Tom, my teammate. He kicked the soccer ball toward me. The other team's players, in their red uniforms, charged. But I got to the ball first.

I broke into a run with the ball. As I ran, I glanced at the crowd. Yes, my grandfather was watching! Finally, I had a chance to show him what I could do.

I'd just met my Japanese grandfather for the first time. Two weeks before, he'd said his farewells to Japan. Then he moved to America to live with us.

I wanted to get to know my grandfather. But I don't speak Japanese, so we couldn't talk to each other. That's why I wanted to play a good soccer game while he was watching. I wanted to make him proud of me.

As I ran toward the goal, some kids in red uniforms tried to block me. I kicked the ball past them and kept going. With only a few seconds left to play, our team was behind by one point. I got close enough to the goal to shoot. I aimed the ball. I pulled back my leg to kick. Then, suddenly, I fell flat on my face on the muddy ground.

The goalie scooped up the ball in triumph and kicked it away. I sat up. A loose shoelace trailed away from my right shoe. I'd tripped over my own shoelace!

That was the end for our team. The last
few seconds of the game ticked away. The
final whistle blew. The red team cheered and
slapped each others' hands in triumph,
looking vain and proud.

I got up slowly, feeling awful. We'd lost the
game. I'd fallen on my face. Instead of feeling
proud of me, my grandfather would be
ashamed.

When we got home, I ran upstairs to my room. I closed the door and flopped miserably on my bed. A few minutes later, there was a knock at the door.

"Come in," I said glumly.

Grandfather walked in with a wooden box. My dad and mom were right behind him. They were all smiling.

"Grandfather wants to give you a gift for Children's Day," Dad explained. "Today is the fifth of May. In Japan, that's a holiday on which families honor their children."

I sat up on the bed and tried to smile. I knew a present wouldn't comfort me. I was too old for that. But I didn't want to hurt Grandfather's feelings.

Grandfather smiled at me while he lifted off the lid. His smile was wide, like my dad's. I wanted to smile back, but I couldn't. I still felt too bad about the game.

I felt worse when I saw what he took out of the box. In a rustle of silk, Grandfather proudly held up the gift for me to see. It was a doll.

A doll! I couldn't believe it. Didn't my grandfather know that most boys my age don't have dolls? I had to work hard to keep from frowning.

"Dad," I said. "Please tell Grandfather I don't play with dolls."

Then I saw the look on my father's face. He touched the doll's silk robe. "I haven't seen this since I left Japan. This isn't just any doll, Yuji. It's a traditional Japanese doll."

"It looks like a doll to me," I said unhappily. Then I looked carefully at the doll's golden helmet and his robe. I saw his strong, vain face. He looked like a proud, brave soldier.

"This doll is a noble Japanese soldier, Yuji," said Mom.

"Right," said Dad. "On Children's Day, families display dolls to honor their sons. This is the doll that my family displayed for me when I was a boy."

Grandfather said something in Japanese, and my father translated.

"Grandfather says that when he said his farewells to Japan, he didn't say farewell to Japan's traditions," my father explained. "He wants you to have the doll because you are his family. He says that when you played soccer today, you were strong and bold, just like our ancestors."

I stood up, feeling my face turn red. "No, I wasn't." I spoke straight to Grandfather. "I fell down. I missed the shot. We lost the game."

Grandfather nodded as if he understood, even before Dad told him what I'd said. He spoke, and Dad translated.

"Grandfather says that even Japanese warriors didn't always win their battles. But they didn't give up."

I looked from the doll's small, fierce face to my grandfather's broad, kind one. We still couldn't talk to each other. But it was easy for me to understand the pride in Grandfather's eyes. Slowly, inside me, the pain of losing the game melted away.

"Thank you, Grandfather," I said, and I took the doll out of his hands.

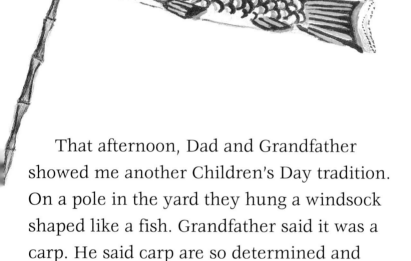

That afternoon, Dad and Grandfather showed me another Children's Day tradition. On a pole in the yard they hung a windsock shaped like a fish. Grandfather said it was a carp. He said carp are so determined and strong that they can swim up waterfalls.

All afternoon, the carp danced in the wind like a fish swimming upstream. Inside, the samurai doll stood guard.

In all the rest of our games that spring, we played great soccer. Grandfather saw us win many games. He saw me score goals too. Whether we won or lost, I knew that my grandfather was proud of me. Whenever I played, I tried to be as strong and determined as the carp and the doll.